ISLE OF WIGHT ALBUMS REVISITED

100 Years of Island Photographs from the 1880s to the 1980s

By
Alan Stroud

Best Wishes

Alan Stroud

Now and Then Books © 2018

Isle Of Wight Albums Revisited

Acknowledgements

The vast majority of the photographs in this book have come from my own collection but some have been provided by friends who I need to thank.

Firstly I would like to thank John Groves of Cowes Heritage Society for kindly allowing the use of some of his photographs. John was instrumental in forming the Cowes Heritage Society which is now home to an important collection of historical documents and artefacts relating to Cowes. Aided by his wife Maureen, John deserves all our thanks for spending many, many hours over the years in encouraging the collection and preservation of this material.

In 1967 my lifelong friend Colin Fairweather had the good sense to photograph the death throes of Newport railway station. My thanks go to him for allowing the use of some of his historic photos.

My cousin Geoff White is the owner of a remarkable collection of photographs taken by our grandfather, Alfred Arnold, in the first years of the 20th century. Although neither of us knew our grandfather, we are sure he would be pleased and proud to see his photographs in print. I am grateful to Geoff for making them available for this book.

I also need to thank Gay Baldwin, Richard Brimson, Alan Dinnis, Rob Martin and Tim Wander, who all assisted with captions or photographs.

Finally, thanks go to my wife, Sue, for supporting me in everything I do.

Printed by Short Run Press
Bittern Road
Sowton Industrial Estate
Exeter
EX2 7LW

Published by Now and Then Books IW © Alan Stroud 2018.
Artwork and layout : Alan Stroud
E-mail: nowandthenbooksiw@googlemail.com

ISBN 978-0-9565076-9-3

There are one hundred years of photographs in this book. They were taken by all manner of photographers on all manners of equipment. The first photographs were taken using glass plate negatives and the last ones were taken on 35mm celluloid film. In some cases the identity of the photographer is known whilst others remain anonymous. Whether they took their photographs for commercial purposes or simply for their own pleasure, the photographers all had the same intention - to capture a moment in time. Some had posterity in mind, others just the fleeting moment but what they all have in common is that their work has managed to survive - in some cases nearly 140 years after they clicked their shutter. This book revisits their work and celebrates their art.

The photographs are presented in chronological order, decade by decade. In every case they have been produced from the original glass plate, roll film negative or slide, the caption for each photograph detailing which format it has been produced from.

The majority of the photographs in the early part of the book were taken using 'half-plate' glass negatives, 6½ by 4¾ inch sheets of thin glass coated with light sensitive emulsion. They were bulky, heavy and very fragile but produced superb results capturing detail in a quality still unmatched by today's digital cameras.

Many of the early half-plate photographs were taken by WR (William) Hogg of Ryde, a name well known to Island postcard collectors. Hogg, a highly skilled photographer, took the photographs in the early 1900s to produce postcards which he then sold from his sub-post office at the bottom of George Street in Ryde. His elegant half-plate camera, made of brass-bound hardwood, with leather bellows, was large and unwieldy and Hogg had to contend with long exposure times meaning the camera had to be mounted on a cumbersome tripod. On arrival at the scene to be photographed, Mr Hogg's camera (see example opposite) needed elaborate preparation and setting up before he could take a single photograph – instant snapshots were out of the question. However, all that was to change with the arrival of the roll-film camera.

One of the most popular and successful roll-film cameras of its day was the 'Kodak Brownie' box camera, introduced in 1901. One of the first 'compact cameras', it sold in its millions. A selection of Brownie 2¼" × 3¼" negatives from 1906 are included in the book. They were taken by Alfred Arnold, the grandfather of myself and my cousin, Geoff White, who is the owner of these and many other negatives taken by Alfred.

The discovery of some 1940s colour positives was a rare find. Sixteen of them are included here allowing us to see the Island in colour nearly 80 years ago. They are the work of Newport professional, C.A. White, taken on *Dufaycolor* film, which he processed himself. Introduced in 1935, Dufaycolor's strength was that it was affordable for amateurs but technically it was no match for its rival, *Kodachrome*, and it was discontinued in the early 1950s.

The next major sequence of photographs date from the summer of 1941 and are of the Saro laminated wood factory, adjacent to the Folly Inn on the east side of the River Medina. The plates are part of a collection of over 60 superb quality 'whole-plate' glass negatives measuring 8½ x 6½ inches. They were commissioned by Saro for use in a promotional book and were taken by an unknown professional photographer.

Similarly, the series of high quality 3 x 3 inch glass negatives taken in JS White's shipyard at Cowes are also clearly the work of a professional but the reason for taking these photographs is unknown. They have not appeared in print until now.

The JS White and CA White photographs were produced in 3 x 3 inch or 2¼ x 2¼ inch size respectively, on either film or glass plate. Both sets of photographs are presented here in their original square format.

In the 1960s through to the 1980s, Frederick Coundley of Cowes, a keen amateur photographer, took hundreds of photographs around the Island. Some of his negatives, both black and white and colour, have kindly been made available by John Groves.

My late father-in-law, Harry Matthews, took the photographs of the 1970 festival at Afton. He would be pleased to see them in print.

The book ends with a series of photographs of various Island scenes produced from a mixture of original 35mm black and white negatives and colour slides. They are taken from the collections of various photographers, including the author who in those days used a Nikon Nikkormat 35mm camera.

Most of the photographs speak for themselves but some benefit from a little explanation. Rather than put any captions on the photo pages, notes on relevant photographs will be found at the back of the book.

The dating of photographs can be fraught with danger. For that reason the photographs are presented in the safer format of decade by decade. However, where a precise date is known for any photograph, it has been included in the caption.

Hopefully this collection will serve two purposes. Firstly, it will be a reminder for some of the older generation amongst us of how some things used to be, and secondly it is a reminder for the current generation that they should be out photographing and recording their surroundings for posterity just as the photographers in these pages did.

A building or landmark that has stood for hundreds of years can disappear in a morning. What is familiar and commonplace today will not always be so.

Alan Stroud, 2018.

3" x 3" glass lantern slide

Plate 1: Carisbrooke From The Castle

3" x 3" glass lantern slide

Plate 2: Yarmouth Square

3" x 3" glass lantern slide

Plate 3: Carisbrooke Ford

Plate 4: Carisbrooke High Street

3" x 3" glass lantern slide

WR Hogg : 6½" x 4¾" glass plate negative

Plate 5: Ryde Esplanade

WR Hogg : 6½" x 4¾" glass plate negative

Plate 6: Ryde Esplanade

Plate 7: Western Esplanade, Ryde, By Night

WR Hogg : 6½" x 4¾" glass plate negative

WR Hogg : 6½" x 4¾" glass plate negative

Plate 8: Western Esplanade Sands, Ryde

Plate 9: Eastern Esplanade Gardens, Ryde

WR Hogg : 6½" x 4¾" glass plate negative

Anon : 6½" x 4¾" glass plate negative

Plate 10: Afton Manor, 1904

Plate 11: Afton Manor, 1904

Anon : 6½" x 4¾" glass plate negative

Anon : 6½" x 4¾" glass plate negative

Plate 12: Afton Manor, 1904

Plate 13: Edwardian Picnic

Anon : 6½″ x 4¾″ glass plate negative

Alfred Arnold : 3½" x 2½"roll film negative

Plate 14: Bridge Square, East Cowes, 1906

Plate 15: Blacksmith and Coalman's Cart, 1906

Alfred Arnold : 3½" x 2½" roll film negative

Alfred Arnold : 3½" x 2½"roll film negative

Plate 16: Cowes Regatta, 1907

Plate 17: Soldiers Bathing At Fort Albert, Colwell

Toogood : 6½" x 4¾" glass plate negative

Toogood : 6½ x 4¾ glass plate negative

Plate 18: Edinburgh Regiment At Unknown West Wight Location

Anon : 6½" x 4¾" glass plate negative

Plate 19: Cowes Esplanade and Pier

Plate 20: Coronation Fleet Review, 1911

Hughes and Mullins : Detail from 12" x 10" glass plate negative

Plate 21: Spithead Hotel, Bembridge

WR Hogg : 6½" x 4¾" glass plate negative

WR Hogg : 6½" x 4¾" glass plate negative

Plate 22: Ryde Pier Entrance, April 1912

Plate 23: Seaview Pier From Seagrove Bay

WR Hogg : 6½" x 4¾" glass plate negative

WR Hogg : 6½" x 4¾" glass plate negative

Plate 24: Advertisement Hoardings, Railway Line, Ryde St Johns

Plate 25: Yaverland Road, Sandown, 1920

Toogood : 6½" x 4¾" glass plate negative

Anon : 6½" x 4¾" glass plate negative

Plate 26: Site of Fishbourne Ferry Terminal, Wootton Creek, 1925

Plate 27: Isle of Wight Rifles' Camp

Anon : 6½" x 4¾" glass plate negative

Anon : 6½" x 4¾" glass plate negative

Plate 28: Blackgang Chine

Plate 29: Hope Beach, Shanklin

Toogood : 6½" x 4¾" glass plate negative

Toogood : 6½" x 4¾" glass plate negative

Plate 30: Steephill Cove

CA White : 2½" x 3½" negative

Plate 31: Team of Horses With Roller

Plate 32: Hay Turning

CA White : 2½" x 3½" negative

CA White : 3″x 3″ glass plate negative

Plate 33: Newport Harbour

CA White : 3" x 3" glass plate negative

Plate 34: 'The Match' Passing Through Railway Drawbridge, Newport Harbour

CA White : 3" x 3" glass plate negative

Plate 35: Cement Mills, Dodnor

CA White : 3" x 3" glass plate negative

Plate 36: Man and Carthorse, Unknown Location

CA White : 3" x 3" glass plate negative

Plate 37: Cottage, 11 Barrington Row, (Winkle Street), Calbourne

CA White : 2¼" x 2¼" positive colour film

Plate 38: Barrington Row, (Winkle Street), Calbourne

CA White : 2¼" x 2¼" positive colour film

Plate 39: Cement Mills, Dodnor

CA White : 2¼" x 2¼" positive colour film

Plate 40: River Medina From East Bank, Looking Towards Newport

CA White : 2¼" x 2¼" positive colour film

Plate 41: Blackhouse Quay

CA White : 2¼″ x 2¼″ positive colour film

Plate 42: Foreshore, Blackhouse Quay

CA White : 2¼" x 2¼" positive colour film

Plate 43: Railway Drawbridge, Newport Harbour

CA White : 2¼″ x 2¼″ positive colour film

Plate 44: In The Garden

CA White : 2¼" x 2¼" positive colour film

Plate 45: Horse Drawn Reaper

CA White : 2¼″ x 2¼″ positive colour film

Plate 46: Family And Harvest

CA White : 2¼" x 2¼" positive colour film

Plate 47: Stooks Of Gathered Oats

CA White : 2¼" x 2¼" positive colour film

Plate 48: Campion And Bluebells, Unknown Location

Plate 49: Shepherd

CA White : 2¼″ x 2¼″ positive colour film

CA White : 2¼" x 2¼" positive colour film

Plate 50: Lower Shide Mill, Newport

CA White : 2¼" x 2¼" positive colour film

Plate 51: West Mill, Newport

CA White : 2¼″ x 2¼″ positive colour film

Plate 52: Two Young Women

CA White : 2¼" x 2¼" positive colour film

Plate 53: Jubilee Stores, Newport Harbour

Toogood : 6½" x 4¾" glass plate negative

Plate 54: Colwell Bay

Toogood : 6½" x 4¾" glass plate negative

Plate 55: Brambles Holiday Camp, Freshwater

Toogood : 6½″ x 4¾″ glass plate negative

Plate 56: Freshwater Bay

Plate 57: Saro 'Lorries Outside Old Store,' 1941

Anon : 6½" x 4¾" glass plate negative

Anon : 6½″ x 4¾″ glass plate negative

Plate 58: Saro Factory, June 12, 1941

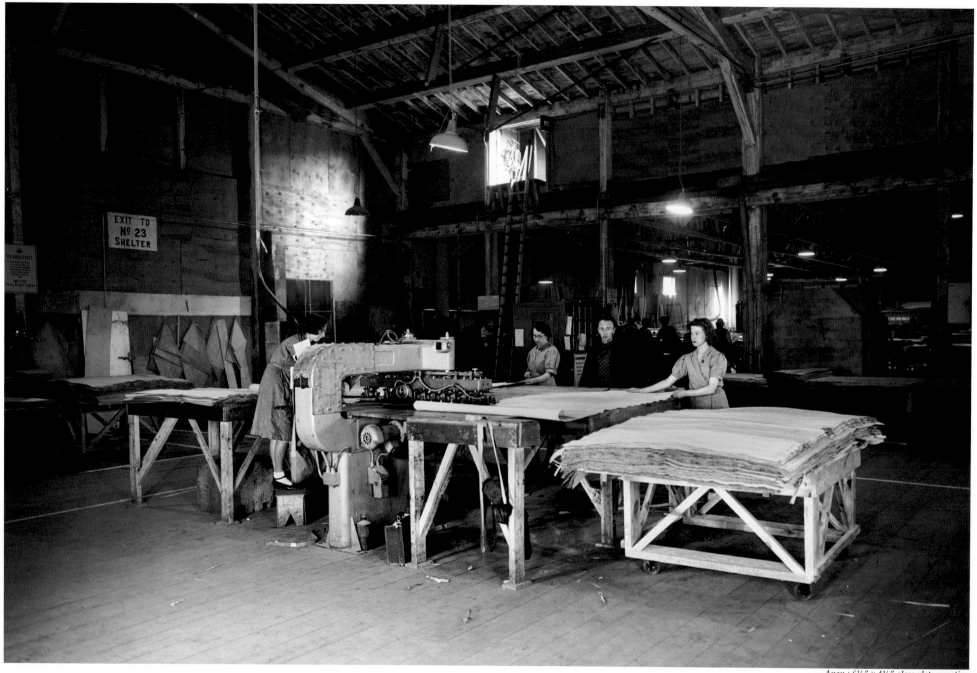

Plate 59: Saro Works, June 12, 1941

Anon : 6½" x 4¾" glass plate negative

Anon : 6½" x 4¾" glass plate negative

Plate 60: Saro 'Walrus Aircraft Assembly Frames,' June 18, 1941

Plate 61: Saro Works, June 18, 1941

Anon : 6½" x 4¾" glass plate negative

Anon : 6½" x 4¾" glass plate negative

Plate 62: The Folly Inn, 1941

Anon : 35mm negative. © C. Fairweather

Plate 63: Cowes Railway Station

Anon : 35mm negative. © C. Fairweather

Plate 64: Newport Station And Former Line to Freshwater

Anon : 3" x 3" glass plate positive

Plate 65: Forging Press, JS White's Foundry

Anon : 3" x 3" glass plate positive

Plate 66: Casting, JS White's Foundry

Anon : 3" x 3" glass plate positive

Plate 67: JS White's Laying Out Loft, Falcon Yard, East Cowes

Anon : 3" x 3" glass plate positive

Plate 68: RMS Caesarea Under Construction, Falcon Yard Slipway, East Cowes

Anon : 3" x 3" glass plate positive

Plate 69: RMS Caesarea Fitting Out, 1961

Coundley : 35mm negative

Plate 70: RMS Caesarea and Sarnia, 1961

Plate 71: Ventnor Station

Plate 72: Ventnor Station, 1964

Coundley : 35mm negative

Plate 73: Ryde Bound Train Drawing Into Sandown Station

Coundley : 35mm negative

Coundley : 35mm negative

Plate 74: Mill Hill Station, Cowes, 1965

Plate 75: Newport Station, 1965

Anon : *35mm negative.* © *C. Fairweather*

Plate 76: Ryde Bound Train Leaving Newport Station, 1965

Colin Fairweather : 2¼″ x 2¼″ negative

Plate 77: Newport North Signal Box Demolition, 1967

Colin Fairweather : 2¼″ x 2¼″ negative

Plate 78: Scrapped Rolling Stock, Newport Station, 1967

Coundley : 35mm negative

Plate 79: Spring Tide Flood, Victoria Arms, Brunswick Road, Cowes

Plate 80: Princess Flying Boat, Medina Road, Cowes

Plate 81: Cowes, 1969

Anon : 10" x 10" negative

Anon : 10" x 10" negative

Plate 82: East Cowes, 1969

Anon : 10" x 10" negative

Plate 83: Newport, 1972

Plate 84: Cowes High Street, 1972

Alan Stroud : 35mm negative

Plate 85: The Royal Oak, Terminus Road, Cowes

Anon: 35mm negative

Alan Stroud : 35mm colour slide

Plate 86: Odessa Boatyard, Little London, Newport

Harry Matthews : 35mm colour slide

Plate 87: Isle of Wight Festival, Afton, August 1970

Plate 88: Isle of Wight Festival, Afton, August 1970

Plate 89: Isle of Wight Festival, Afton, August 1970

Harry Matthews : 35mm colour slide

Harry Matthews : 35mm colour slide

Plate 90: Cowes Railway Station Following Closure, 1972

Plate 91: Demolition of Sea Street Warehouses, 1972

Harry Matthews : 35mm colour slide

Alan Stroud : 35mm colour slide

Plate 92: Demolition of Warehouses, Site of Bargemans Rest, 1972

Plate 93: Lugley Street, Newport, 1972

Alan Stroud : 35mm colour slide

Harry Matthews : 35mm colour slide

Plate 94: Crocker Street, Newport, 1972

Alan Stroud : 35mm colour slide

Plate 95: Towngate Mill Buildings, Lower St James Street, Newport, 1972

Plate 96: Malt and Hops, Orchard Street, Newport

Reg Davies : 35mm colour slide

Plate 97: Newport Harbour

Plate 98: Newport Harbour

Reg Davies : 35mm colour slide

Alan Stroud : 35mm colour slide

Plate 99: Cowes Road, Northwood, February 1978

Reg Davies : 35mm colour slide

Plate 100: Ventnor Coach Station,

Reg Davies : 35mm colour slide

Plate 101: Newport Bus Station, South Street

Reg Davies : 35mm colour slide

Plate 102: Ryde Esplanade Bus Station

Ron Morris : 35mm colour slide

Plate 103: Ryde Hospital, Swanmore Road

Ron Morris : 35mm colour slide

Plate 104: Railway Carriage Beach Huts, St Helens

Plate 105: Denmark Road School, Cowes

Coundley : 2½" x 3½" negative

Coundley : 2½″ x 3½″ negative

Plate 106: Denmark Road, Cowes

Coundley : 2½″ x 3½″ negative

Plate 107: Cowes Chain Ferry

Coundley : 2½" x 3½" negative

Plate 108: Victoria Road Post Office, Cowes

Plate 109: The Last Ever Newport Market, December 1983

Alan Stroud : 35mm colour slide

Plate 110: Newport High Street, 1983

Plate 111: Jukes Hardware Store, St Thomas Square, Newport, 1983

Plate 112: 19, St James Square, June 1983

Plate 113: St James Square, Newport, 1983

Alan Stroud : 35mm negative

Plate 114: St Thomas Square, Newport, 1983

Alan Stroud : 35mm negative

Plate 115: Cowes, 1983

Plate 116: East and West Cowes, 1983

Anon : 35mm negative

Plate 117: Newport, 1983

Anon : 35mm negative

Plate 118: Carisbrooke Village, 1983

Plate 119: Ventnor and Pier, 1983

Anon : 35mm negative

Plate 120: Shanklin Pier, 1983

Plate 121: Brighstone Village and Tea Gardens, 1983

Alan Stroud : 35mm negative

Plate 122: View From St Thomas Church Tower, 1983

Plate 123: Horsebridge Hill, 1983

Plates 1 to 4 are from a collection of 60 lantern slides originally sold as a boxed set. They were intended to be projected for an audience and came with a booklet providing the projectionist with a commentary for each slide. The booklet refers to "the recent royal marriage at Whippingham," a reference to the 1885 marriage of Princess Beatrice, while in the photograph of Carisbrooke village the railway line, opened in 1888, does not appear.

Plates 10, 11 and 12, Afton Manor, were taken in the grounds of Afton Manor, owned at that time by the Cheverton family of Cheverton Motors, Newport. Someone in the family owned a high quality glass plate camera and nearly 40 superb quality glass plates exist showing not only the grounds but many of the vehicles the family owned.

Plates 14, 15 and 16 were taken by Alfred Arnold, the author's grandfather, on a Brownie 620 camera. A coppersmith at Saunders-Roe, Alfred was a keen amateur photographer, processing his own negatives. The central figure in **Plate 15** is probably Alfred's adoptive father, George Arnold, blacksmith of East Cowes and latterly, Newport.

Plate 17, Soldiers, shows the soldiers of Fort Albert about to take a naked swim in the sea. By the time this photograph was taken in the early 1900s the Fort had long ceased to have any defensive purpose and had been downgraded to barracks status. It was only finally decommissioned in 1957.

Plate 26, Fishbourne Creek, appeared in the *County Press* edition of March 8th 1925, captioned "The site chosen for the new ferry terminal at Fishbourne."

Plates 31 to 53 are part of a large collection of black and white glass plates and rare colour positives of the Island taken in the 1940s by CA White, a photographer who traded from East Cowes. A large number of them have clearly been entered in photographic competitions and bear the address, '57 Medina Avenue, Newport.' They are labelled with whimsical, romantic titles for competition purposes which, frustratingly, do not reveal the location of a single photograph. Some locations are obvious but many of the scenes, especially of rural cottages, still need identifying.

Plate 35, Cement Mills: Alan Dinnis, author of *West Medina Cement Mill*, published in 2016, gives a date of perhaps the late 1940s for this photograph and Alan suspects the sailing barge in **Plate 39** is almost certainly the cement company's barge, 'Medina'.

Plate 42, Foreshore, Blackhouse Quay: This view can be seen today through a gap in the hedge in the car park of Odessa Boatyard, looking towards Cowes. Turning towards Newport then gives the view seen in **Plate 53.**

Plates 45, 46 and 47 were taken at an unknown location. Frustratingly, Mr White has simply labelled the plates 'Harvest Time'. Similarly, the gentleman in **Plate 49** remains anonymous, being identified only as 'The Shepherd.' The two young ladies in **Plate 52** share a similar fate as does the lady in **Plate 44.**

Plate 50, Lower Shide Mill: The Mill stood in what is now St George's Way, at its junction with Pan Lane. The railway line into nearby Shide station can just be seen in the distance.

Plate 51, West Mill: The mill building can be seen today, surrounded by modern housing, alongside public footpath N58 at the bottom of Wellington Road, Newport. (Please note : Some of these colour photographs exhibit 'interference patterns' due to the nature of the film base.)

Plates 57 to 62 show the 'Saro Laminated Wood Products' factory, adjacent to the Folly Inn. They are part of a collection of 60 high quality 8½" x 6½" glass 'whole plate' negatives taken in 1941 by an unknown professional. They were commissioned to illustrate a 50 page book, *Saro Plywood*, published in 1946 to announce to the trade that Saro was back in business after five years of war work making aircraft wings. The plates record the factory interiors and also the grounds, including the newly built air raid shelters and look-out posts.

Plate 64, Former Line To Freshwater, shows the Freshwater railway line leaving Newport railway station on its way to the bottom of Hunny Hill where it crossed the road on a bridge to make its way to Yarmouth and Freshwater. Following closure in 1956, these tracks became sidings.

Plates 65 to 69 are part of a collection of sixteen professionally taken photographs of JS White's shipyard in 1961. The negatives were converted to positive glass slides for use in a projector. The purpose remains unknown. The Caesarea, launched January 1960, and Sarnia launched in September the same year, were passenger ferries on the Weymouth to Channel Isles run until the mid-1970s. After service with various new owners the Caesarea was scrapped in 1986 and the Sarnia the following year.

Plates 72 - 74, 79, 80 and Plates 108 to 111, in colour, are part of a collection of hundreds of photographs taken by Frederick Coundley, an amateur photographer of Cowes.

Plate 73, Sandown Station, shows pupils of Sandown Grammar School just about to board the incoming Ryde-bound train for their homeward journey. In the 1950s, pupils from as far afield as Cowes took the train to Sandown Grammar each day.

Plates 77 and 78, Newport Station: In the summer of 1967, Colin Fairweather, then 16, had the good sense to photograph the demolition of what until the previous year had been Newport's busy railway station. Colin also captured the scrapping and cutting up of the rolling stock that had been assembled there to go under the cutter's torch. Newport North signal box is now the patch of grass outside Premier Ford on the Riverway Estate.

Plate 80, Princess Flying Boat: In 1946 the government ordered three flying boats from Saunders-Roe, now GKN. Designed to carry 105 passengers in luxury, the Princesses should have taken to the air in 1950 but the engines were found to be underpowered. New ones had to be developed, a task that would take some years, so each craft was filled with eight tons of dessicant and sprayed with a cocoon of nine tons of plastic. Two were towed over to Calshot, while the third one sat on a slipway at Medina Road, Cowes, where it became a local landmark for the next 20 years. While they slept, large efficient jet engines arrived, rendering them unsaleable and they were finally scrapped in 1967.

Plate 85, The Royal Oak: With its beautiful tiled frontage it was one of the few Long's pubs on the Island. After the closure of the Cowes to Ryde railway line in 1966 the whole area was redeveloped and the pub and the nearby railway station were demolished in 1973.

Plates 87 to 89, The 1970 Festival: The 1969 Festival drew 150,000 fans to see Bob Dylan at Wootton. Buoyed by this success, promoters Ray and Ronnie Foulk of Totland, two enterprising brothers in their mid-twenties, put on an even larger festival in 1970 attracting 300,000 fans. Musically, the festival was a huge success but the Freshwater site, (imposed on the brothers by a hostile council) had a fatal flaw – it was, as the council knew only too well, overlooked by Afton Down. To no-one's surprise, especially the council, the option of a free ringside seat had a catastrophic effect on ticket sales, ensuring the festival made a loss

Plates 91 and 92, taken by Harry Matthews, show the scandalous demolition by the same council of Victorian warehouses in Sea Street to make way for a council car park.

Plate 104, Railway Carriage Beach Huts: In 1914 the IW Railway purchased 18 carriages from the Metropolitan Railway of London. In 1928-29 they were withdrawn from service and ten went to St Helens to begin a new life as beach huts where they remain to this day, albeit now   boarded over.

Plate 108, Victoria Road Sub Post Office: One of the last 'corner shops' in Cowes, it was run by Mr and Mrs Greenham for many years. Outside, a poster advertising "Mack and Mabel" at the Shanklin Theatre dates the photo to September or October of 1983.

Plate 112, 19 St James Square, was taken during the 1983 general election campaign when Stephen Ross for the Liberals won the Isle of Wight. David Steele, party leader, peers out from the shop window.

ISLE OF WIGHT ALBUMS REVISITED

Published by Now and Then Books 2018

E-mail: nowandthenbooksiw@googlemail.com